Power I
Made Simple

A beginner's guide to boating

An easy to follow checklist
for preparing,
going boating and
coming home

By

Captain Richard Frankhuizen

April 2014
Updated 2019

Richard Frankhuizen © 2014

Table of Contents

Preparation

"There's nothing . . . absolutely nothing . . . half so much worth doing as simply messing around in boats."

Kenneth Grahame,
The Wind in the Willows (River Rat to Mole)

If you are new to power boating, welcome. You will find that your time with your family and friends will be some of the richest experiences you will ever have. Boating creates wonderful memories and adventures that will be shared for years.

And while there is a lot to learn to be safe and have fun, the objective of this guide to help build confidence so you will look forward to going boating and have a relaxing and fun time.

The term skier is used to identify wake boarder, surfer, single or double skiers or even a knee-boarder or towing an inflatable. Driver and participants will decide what fun you will have today.

The document is a brief checklist for preparing and going boating. There are many excellent sources of information to gain detailed information and expertise on maritime topics. The focus here is to introduce and invite you into the wonderful world of boating, how to make it easy and fun and safe. Welcome to the boating family.

1.1 Boating Skills

Item	Note	Check
Boating Skills	Your toolbox of skills can grow each time you go boating. Ask when you need help and use the state and federal references.	✔
Rules of the Road	The California State Parks, Department of Boating and Waterways. http://www.dbw.ca.gov/ ABCs of California Boating Law The United States Coast Guard Rules of the Road. http://www.navcen.uscg.gov/?pageName=navRulesContent	✔
Knots	There are three basic knots that will help you manage your boat successfully. A cleat hitch, clove hitch and bowline.	✔
Trailering	Towing a trailer takes a little getting used to but driving a bit slower, taking wide turns and all will be well	✔
Launching	Launching causes the most stress for new boaters. When it is your turn. Take your time. If you need help, ask. There are nice people everywhere. No yelling.	✔
Docking	The second most stressful event is learning how to dock the boat. Remember, any landing you can walk away from is a good one.	✔
Language /Definitions	There are many nautical terms to learn which can be fun. Source: An abbreviated list from Wikipedia is at the end http://en.wikipedia.org/wiki/Glossary of nautical terms	✔

1.2 Preparation of the Boat

Item	Note	Check
Make it Easy	Getting the boat ready. There are two aspects to boat preparation. The boat and your personal effects.	✔
Get the boat	Check to see that you have the correct size ball to match the hitch.	✔

Cover	Remove the cover fold the dirty side to the dirty side.	✔
Cushions	Put all the seat cushions back into position.	✔
Gas	Check the fuel level and fill up before going to the lake.	✔
Plug	#1 - Install the plug(s) at home prior to loading gear. Sufficient distractions at home and at the launch make it easy to forget.	✔
Oil	Check the engine and transmission oil levels.	✔
Lines	Bow and stern lines to be able to manage the boat at the dock and to be able tie up.	✔
Fenders	To protect the boat when tied up to the dock or other boats. Rafting up to others on the lake or river can be great fun.	✔
Trailer	Inspect tire pressure, Axle grease, brake and turn signal lights and tie downs.	✔

1.3   Personal Items

Item	Note	Check
Water	Always take bottled water to keep yourself hydrated. Frozen water bottles make great ice cubes. No water mess in the ice chest and they provide drinkable water as they melt.	✔
NO Alcohol	Alcohol and boating do not mix.	✔
Lunch	It is always great to have food on the boat.	✔
Sun screen	We are hoping for sunny weather.	✔
Sunglasses	We are hoping for sunny weather.	✔
Tools	Tools comes in handy from time to time.	✔

Camera	Take lots of pictures.	✓
Cash	Pay for the launch, buy gas, go out to lunch or dinner.	✓
Life Jackets	There needs to be a life jacket that fits each passenger on board.	✓
Ski Flag	Small Red Flag that is used to signal that you have a skier and line in the water.	✓
Skis, wake or surf boards, inflatables	Load the skiing toys into the boat	✓
Binding Slim / Soap	A little binding slim or dish soap makes it easy. A little spray bottle with a 50/50 water to soap works well.	✓
Towels	It is always nice to wrap up in a dry towel	✓
Dry clothes	It is always nice to get out of wet clothes.	✓
Cell phone	Cell phones are put in a dry location. Handy when emergency services are needed	✓
Paper towels	It is better than using one's towel to clean off grease, food or oil, etc.	✓
Quart zip lock bags	Perfect for left-over food	✓
Trash Bags	Perfect for trash. ☺	✓
First Aid Kit	Have a first aid kit on the boat always.	✓
Boat Towels	Two or three old towels used for wiping the boat down to remove water spots and the bath tub ring at the water line. Wipe down right after pulling the boat out of the water and is still wet.	✓

1.4 Fueling

Item	Note	Check
Fuel	Always make sure you have sufficient fuel for your boating adventure. There are typically two places to get fuel, the gas station or the fuel dock at the marina. Fuel at the gas station is always less expensive.	✔
Gas Station	Fuel the boat like you would fuel a car. Do not over fill. Fuel will come out the fuel vent if you do. Wipe off the excess fuel off your gel coat finish.	✔
Drive to Marina	As you are towing your boat, the vents on the boat will ventilate the bilge like the blower would.	✔
Once Launched	Turn the blower on anyway, wait, then start your engine.	✔

1.5 Fueling at the Dock

Item	Note	Check
Arrive at Dock	Once at the fuel dock, properly tie the boat up so it is secure. Invite your passengers to stretch their legs, use the restroom, etc. Begin fueling. Once complete stow the fuel line and reinstall the gas cap.	✔
Blower	In the small chance that there are gas fumes in the bilge, it is necessary to run the blower for a few minutes to remove the fumes from the bilge prior to staring the engine. *	✔
Engine Start	After running the blower for a few minutes, then it is okay to start the engine.	✔
Load up	Get all your passengers in the boat and prepare for departure.	✔
Gas Fumes in bilge	*If there are gasoline fumes in the bilge, there may be a fuel leak. If there is a fuel leak, no matter how small, it is imperative that it be repaired and excess fuel cleaned up prior to starting the engine and leaving the dock to go boating.	🚷

1.6 Trailering

Item	Note	Check
Depart	Depart for your destination. Remember we just added a few thousand pounds of boat, gear and passengers. Drive slower than normal and give yourself plenty of room for braking. Even with trailer brakes, it is better to be safe than sorry.	✔
Take wide turns	The inside trailer wheel will cut to the inside. Always check your mirrors and follow the inside trailer wheel.	✔
Use your turn signals	When changing lanes, use your signals as your vehicle is now twice as long and it is possible that you have someone in your blind spot. No erratic lane changes and stay in the slower lanes.	✔
BE patient	No cutting across intersections. Wait until you have sufficient time to pull across. Remember you have a long rig now and it will easily block several lanes of traffic.	✔

2 Boating

2.1 Arrival at the Marina

Item	Note	Check
Yay!	You have arrived at your destination.	✔
Pay to launch	This is always a mystery. Some places have a ticket booth, others a guy on bike who pedals around on a bike. Some use a golf cart. Not to worry, if you don't see anyone, start prepping your boat, they will come and find you. And if they don't, ask a fellow boater. Someone will know.	✔
Find a place to park	Find a place to park that puts you in line but does not block the ramp. Prepare your boat for launching.	✔
Bathroom Break	Last chance before heading out. Take advantage of the opportunity.	✔

2.2 Prep for Launching

Item	Note	Check
Check the plug	Double check that the plug is installed and is properly tightened.	✔
Remove the tie straps	Remove the tie straps from the back of the boat	✔
Transfer all gear	Put all the remaining gear from the car into the boat	✔
Prepare dock lines	Attach the bow and stern lines for boat management at the dock.	✔
Install fenders	Set fenders if so desired. This can be optional depending on your crew and how long you will be at the dock.	✔

| Turn on the battery | Turn on the battery switch, DO NOT START the engine. | ✔ |
| Life Jackets | Kiddies put on the life jackets prior to launching the boat or going onto the dock. | ✔ |

2.3 Launching

Item	Note	Check
Line Up	When it is your turn, line up the car and trailer to back down the launch ramp. Passengers are on the dock to assist with launching.	✔
Back the trailer	It is your turn so take your time. Back down slowly. Everyone will wait.	✔
Disconnect the winch	With the boat touching the water – Stop. Disconnect the winch hook from the bow eye.	✔
Boat floats off of the trailer	Continue backing down the ramp. The boat will float easily off the trailer. Your passengers and guests will use the bow and stern lines to maneuver the boat to the dock.	✔
Drive forward	Move slowly up the ramp allowing the water to displace around the trailer. Tires are wet, brakes maybe as well, drive slow.	✔
Parking	Find a location to park your car and trailer and head back to the boat to begin your day of boating. Congratulations, you have launched your boat	✔

2.4   At the Dock

Item	Note	Check
Boat is in the water	Boat is floating and the driver pulls up to park the car and trailer.	✔
Move Boat	Move the boat as far as possible to the rear of the dock away from the launch ramp to allow others to launch while you are waiting for your driver to arrive. This allows others to begin launching.	✔
Start the engine	Run the blower for safety. Have all passengers on the dock when the boat is first started. Listen for odd noises. If the raw water pump impellor is failing the exhaust note will become louder.	✔
Passengers load up	Passengers enter the boat and find a seat. Children under 13 must don a life jacket at all times. About 60% of the public does not know how to swim. Ask your adult guests if they know how to swim and if they would like to wear a life jacket.	✔
Keys, Wallets, Phones	Put all wallets, phones and keys in the glove box or other dry location. Or they will soon go swimming. It happens.	✔
Untie and depart	One or two people remain on the dock to untie the boat. Once untied, they climb in and sit down. The driver checks to see that everyone is sitting down before putting the boat in gear to depart.	✔
Greater than 5 mph	Once out of the 5mph zone, allow the engine to warm up, check for other boats and traffic and that children are sitting before increasing speed. Kids get excited and tend to get up on their knees. Say "bottoms down", kids seem to understand and typically respond.	✔
Enjoy the	Go the appropriate speed for the loading condition of the boat and water conditions.	✔

ride		
Look Behind You	Why? Looking out at the water from the land looks different than looking at the land from the water. At the end of the day when you attempt to come back to the marina, you will not recognize the shoreline. So, as you leave, look behind you to see the place you just left.	✓

2.5 Underway and your wake

Item	Note	Check
Wake	The wake is the wave that the boat produces when the boat is underway. There are three primary wake sizes: No wake, large wake and small wake.	✓
No Wake	The boat is not moving or the boat is in gear and moving at the slowest speed setting which is less than 5 mph. It is the speed at which one travels in a marina, around other boats, swimmers etc.	✓
Large Wake	Most recreational power boats have planning hulls. This means that there will be a transition from displacement (at rest or slow speed) to planning (at speed) and is called plowing. Plowing is when the bow rises as speed is increased. Plowing creates the largest wake. It is necessary to plow to get onto plane, so all planning hull boats will experience this transition in boat performance. As the bow comes back down, the boat is on plane and wake size becomes smaller. Do not slow down to a plow around other boat or swimmers as they will be impacted by that large wake. Either maintain speed or slow down to 5 mph or idling speed to keep the wake that follows to a manageable size.	🚫

Small Wake	After a boat is on plane, the wake will become smaller and is the wake size slalom skiers prefer.	

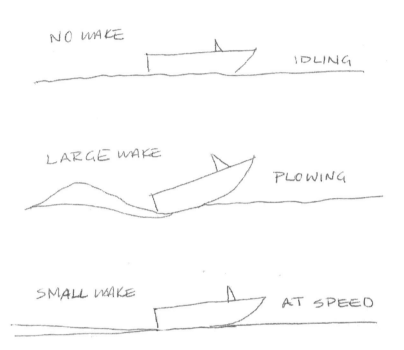

Large Wake for Wake Surfing / Wake Boarding	With wake surfing and wake boarding becoming more popular, boat designs include hull shapes and devices to make a large wake for those participants. This is a necessary part of that sport. Boat drivers need to be aware that they are responsible for any damage that the boat's wake may cause another vessel.	

2.6 On the Lake

Item	Note	Check
Underway	Driving on a lake is a little different than on a river. On a large body of water, boaters tend to go in all kinds of directions. This translates to the Driver having to monitor 360 degrees of traffic when driving. Always look around and behind you before making turns. One never knows if a jet ski or a faster boat is trying to pass you.	✔
Changing course	Always look behind you before making turns. One never knows if a jet ski or a faster boat is trying to pass you	✔
Stopping	Always look behind you before stopping, one never knows if someone is tailgating.	✔
Swimming	Whether in a 5-mph zone or the middle of the lake, swimming is great. Display the red flag to communicate there are people in the water around the boat.	✔

2.7 On the River

Item	Note	Check
Underway	Driving a boat on a river is much like driving on a road. The levees act as lines on the road and people tend to drive on the right side. When pulling a skier, go right down the middle. When an oncoming boat appears, you can veer to the right as you pass. Always look behind you before making turns or changing lanes on the river.	✔
Changing course	Always look around and behind you before making turns. One never knows if a jet ski or a faster boat is trying to pass.	✔
Stopping	Always look behind you before stopping, one never knows if someone is tail-gating.	✔
Swimming	Rivers often do not make great places to swim due to boating traffic. Always be careful and display the red flag to communicate there are	✔

	people in the water.	
Skiing	Pull your skier down the middle of the River. The tendency is to drive on the right like driving a car, but this may get your skier too close to shore.	✔

2.8 At Anchor

Item	Note	Check
Anchor Time	When it is time for lunch or a swim one can float in the lake or river or put out an anchor to keep the boat in one relative location. Relative location is due to the boat swinging around the anchor from the effects of wind and current, presuming that the anchor is set correctly.	✔
Anchor	The device that digs into the bottom of the lake or river to hold your boat in position. You may find it interesting that modern cruise liners do not use anchors. They have dynamic positioning (DP) system which is A GPS based computerized anchoring system. It senses small movements in the vessel location and activates the bow and stern thrusters to keep the vessel exactly where it is programed to stay.	✔
Anchor Scope	Scope is the amount of line to let out versus the depth. A typical scope ratio is 7:1 for strong wind and current. For every 1 foot of depth, 7 feet of line is let out. If the depth is 10 feet, then 70 feet of line is let out. More scope translates to a stronger hold. If you have 70 feet of scope out, the swing of the boat will be 140 feet in diameter. Have an adequate amount of space between you and the next boat. If on a lake that has no current and little or no wind or tidal change, a 4 to 5:1 scope will be plenty for lunch and play time.	✔
Chain	The chain rode is a length of chain between the anchor and the line. The rode adds weight to the line to keep the force of the pull parallel	✔

	to the bottom of the lake. It helps maintain a strong hold.	
Line	Attached to the anchor	✔
Bitter End	Secure the bitter end to the boat to keep the entire system from going overboard and to the bottom. The bitter end is the lose end of the line.	✔
Setting the Anchor	The deploy the anchor, make sure the bitter end is secure (tied to) to the boat, lower the anchor into the water, allow it to hit the bottom, identify about how deep it is (if you do not have a depth sounder) and then let out enough line for your desired scope. Secure the line to a cleat. Put the boat in reverse to pull the anchor across the bottom to make the anchor dig into the bottom. You will feel it grab and the line will become taunt.	✔
At Anchor	Now you are set to relax, take a nap, swim, eat and visit with little concern that your boat will drift away. However, always keep an eye out for changing conditions, shifts in the position of your boat relative to others. Anchors do drag sometimes.	✔

2.9 Docking Considerations

Item	Note	Check
Docking	After launching, docking the boat is the 2nd most stressful boating event. It is not hard. Just go slow, take your time, you will eventually arrive at the dock. With a little practice it will become easier	✔
Docks	Poorly maintained docks can inflict much damage to your boat. Perform a visual inspection for the following; nails or bolts sticking out, worn or missing dock padding, bumpers or cushions. Deploy the fenders	✔
Wind and	When wind and current are a factor, identify what direction the wind is blowing and which way the current is flowing. It is	✔

Current	recommended to drive into the wind and or current to the dock. You will have more control of the boat. You can use the wind to blow you into the dock as well, but in high winds this assistance will accelerate the boat to the dock for a hard landing. One way to mitigate this is to drive into the wind and then make a left or right turn into the docking position. The breeze will put you right where you want to be.	
No wind or current	When there is no wind or current, approach the dock at an angle, say 30 degrees to the final resting position of the boat. Approach slowly while idling or out of gear, when you are almost there turn the wheel away from the dock, put the boat "In gear" and take it "out of gear". Just that fast - In and out. Allow the boat to move, put it in reverse to keep from hitting the dock and bringing the boat speed to zero. When done correctly, someone can step off of the boat and tie off.	✔

2.10 Docking

Item	Note	Check
Approach marina slowly	Look for boat traffic, whose turn is next, etc. Pick where you would like to dock.	✔
Identify Wind and current direction	Identify your wind and current direction.	✔
Determine your docking approach	Knowing where you want to dock and the weather conditions, pick your technique for docking. Upon your turn, take your time.	✔
Prepare	Prepare your dock lines. Everyone will want to help, give them guidance on how	✔

docking lines	they can help.	
Prepare Fenders	Put out your fenders	✔
Visually inspect dock	Visually inspect for anything that might damage your boat.	✔
Approach the dock slowly	Go slow, use the weather, current and the engine to get you where you want to be.	✔
Remove all speed from the boat	Bring the speed of the boat to zero before anyone gets off the boat.	✔
Coming to the Dock	DO NOT depend on passengers to prevent the boat from hitting the dock. They may become injured trying to stop a moving boat from hitting the dock.	🚫
Step from the boat to dock	STEP onto the dock. Never jump.	✔
Tie OFF	Tie off the bow and stern using a cleat hitch. If cleats are available.	✔
Engine OFF	Wait until the boat is tied off before turning off the engine. Something may require you to drive again	✔
Jumping from the boat	Never jump from the boat to dock. Very dangerous.	🚫

3 Pulling People
3.1 Considerations

Item	Note	Check
Safety	The Driver is responsible for the safety of the passengers and crew. When pulling skiers and wake boarders drive down the middle of the river or the middle of finger on a lake. This provides plenty of room on both sides of the boat with distance from the shore for the skier when they fall.	✔
Speed	The tables below outline suggested speeds depending on the age and ability of the participant. For beginners always go slower. It is in the fun of the event that generates good experiences and memories. Going too fast may scare or injure your participants. Going slow always leaves the participant wanting more which is what we Drivers want - more boating fun.	✔
Line taunt	When the Driver is pulling an inflatable, it is imperative to keep the slack out of the line. If the line slacks pull the throttle back to idle immediately. Slack in a line will lead to a jerk impact and may injure your participants.	✔

Age	Tubing or Inflatable - Speed Miles Per Hour
1-5	In gear <5 mph
5-11	8 - 10 mph
9-14	9 - 15 mph
13-16	13 - 20 mph
16-30	15 - 25 mph
30 +	Remember we have to go to work in the morning so be careful

Power Boating Made Simple

Type	Speed Miles Per Hour
Knee Board	5 - 12 mph
Wake Surfing	8-14 mph to generate the ideal surf
Wake Board	12 - 24 mph
Double Skis	10 - 22 mph
Single Ski	24 - 36 mph
Barefooting	36 mph plus

3.2 Hand Signals

Item	Note	Check
Observer	There are a few hand signals for water skiers. It is the observer's job to communicate to the driver which hand signal is being used. The slowest command rules. Boating is about fun, so make it fun, not scary.	✔
Faster	The skier does the thumbs up to request to go faster. The Driver decides if it is safe for both the boat and skier to actually go faster.	✔
Slower	The skier requests to go slower. It is always okay to go slower and the driver should oblige immediately.	✔
Stopping Back to Dock	There are several things that can be done to communicate you wish to stop. Pat yourself on the head or use your hand to signal a cut at your throat. The easiest is to just let go of the rope. The boat will come back for you.	✔
Flag	The Red Flag is displayed to illustrate that there is a ski, skier and or line in the water around the boat.	✔

Driver's Arm up	This is a lost communication. When the Red Flag is displayed by the oncoming boat, once the driver of the oncoming boat sees the line and person in the water, the driver raises his arm to acknowledge that he sees the people and equipment in the water.	✔
Skier Pointing Right or Left	Sometimes the skier knows where to go and will provide direction to the Driver.	✔
Skier Falls, Skier's arm up	When a skier falls, and is OK, will raise one arm to signal to the boat that all is okay.	✔
No Special Rights	A skier behind your boat does not give you special rights. You are bound by the Rules of the Road and in all cases, safety first. This means, slow down and drop the skier if traffic demands.	🚫

3.3 Preparing to pull a skier

Item	Note	Check
Flag	Display flag to communicate that you have a skier and a line in the water.	✔
Line	Used to pull your skier.	✔
Ski	Required unless one is barefooting.	✔
Life Jacket	Always wear a life jacket when skiing.	✔
Engine OFF	Skier dons equipment at the back of the boat or on the swim platform. Enters the water and moves away from the boat and announces that he is clear.	✔
Engine ON	The driver visually checks that the ski line and skier are clear before starting the	✔

	engine and putting it in gear. The observer assists with this duty.	
Preparing to pull skier	Driver puts the boat in gear to take the slack out of the line.	✔
Idle out	Once the slack is out of the line the skier states "Idle Out" or "In Gear". The Driver puts the boat in gear and drags the skier at a slow speed.	✔
Hit it	When the skier is ready the skier states, "Hit it" or "Go" or "Giddy Up" or some other variation of go. The Driver has checked that it is clear of other boating traffic and it is safe to proceed. The Driver provides a gentle but steady acceleration to pull the skier up. Skiers, let the boat do the work. Getting up is more technique than strength.	✔
Falling	All Skiers fall. When a skier falls, pull the throttle back to neutral and allow the boat to slow down. The Observer raises the Red Flag. After the boat slows down, put it in gear and idle around going back to the skier slowly. The Driver takes the skier on the same side as the steering wheel. This allows the Driver to see the skier at all times. Slowing the boat down before turning keeps everything less stressful. Big, fast and hard turns create large wakes, burn fuel and add stress to the day.	✔
Ski again.	You got this. ☺	✔

3.4 Double Skis

Item	Note	Check
Proper Speed	Most boaters pull news skiers way too fast. Opt for the lower part of the speed range. The skier will indicate if they wish to go faster.	✔

3.5 Single Skiing

Item	Note	Check
Proper Speed	Most single skiers will know how fast they wish to ski. Modern ski boats have speed control, like a cruise control, which will regulate the speed of the boat. If available use your speed control, drive in a straight line right down the middle of the river or on the smoothest part of the lake.	✔

3.6 Wake Boarding

Item	Note	Check
Proper Speed	Wakeboarding is another activity that can be pulled on the slower side. Lean toward going to the slow side of the speed range. The boarder will signal if they wish to go faster. Reference the table above for the speed range and opt for the lower part of the speed range.	✔

3.7 Inflatables

Item	Note	Check
Inflatable Safety	Inflatables are easy and fun. But if handled incorrectly can inflict serious injury or death! The driver must never allow the line to acquire slack. Slack in the line will result is a massive jolt. The driver should immediately pull the throttle back to neutral to reduce the impact of the jolt and the tubers should roll off of the inflatable into the water to avoid the jolt impact.	✔
Inflatable Fun	A boat speed of 10-15 mph is all you need for a thrilling ride. With a boat speed of 15 mph and the inflatable on the outside of the arc during a whip is going much faster than the boat. Go slow and make it a fun ride.	✔
Go Slow	Going slow is safer. The goal is to have fun, not injure.	✔

No Slack in the line	Slack in the line will result in a jolt. Riders should roll off of the tube into the water to avoid the jolt.	

4 Going Home
4.1 Trailering the Boat

Item	Note	Check
Back the trailer	Back the trailer into the water at sufficient depth	✔
Boat onto trailer	Using the bow and stern lines, maneuver the boat onto the trailer	✔
Attach the winch	Attach the winch hook to the bow eye. If the trailer is at the correct depth, there will be very little distance to pull the boat forward to the proper resting place on the trailer.	✔
Outdrive	If you have an outboard or inboard / Outboard, raise the unit. This will prevent it from dragging on the ground.	✔
Put the vehicle in Low	Move slowly up the ramp allowing the boat to settle onto the trailer bunks. In many cases the boat will self-correct and properly rest on the trailer.	✔
Boat is out of the water	Stop just above the water, check the back of the boat to verify that the boat is resting properly on the trailer bunks. If not correct, back down slowly, adjust and pull out.	✔
Parking	Find a location off the ramp and out of the way where others can pass and so you can prepare the boat for going home.	✔

4.2 Preparation to go Home

Item	Note	Check
Wipe the boat down	Using the old boat towels, wipe the boat down to remove the bathtub ring at the waterline, water spots and generally clean the boat. Use spray and wax as you wipe the boat down. Wipe down everything, outside, inside, seats, chrome and windshield, etc.	✔

Item	Note	Check
Lines	Coil the ski lines and stow.	✔
Light items	Remove any light items that may blow out of the boat. FYI wet towels will rest nicely on the floor at the driver's seat for the ride home.	✔
Personal Items	Remove all personal items, watches, phones, keys, wallets, purses etc. from the boat and put in the car.	✔
Plug	Remove the plug and stow in the same place each time. This way you will know where it is the next time you go boating.	✔
Life Jackets	Stow in such a way so they do not blow out of the boat.	✔
Battery Switch	Turn the Battery Switch to OFF.	✔
Tie Downs	Install the tie downs at the transom.	✔
Bimini Top	Stow the Bimini top.	✔

4.3 Arriving at Home

Item	Note	Check
Wet items	Remove all wet items from the boat	✔
Personal effects	Remove all personal effects from the boat	✔
Ice chest	Into the kitchen, unfrozen water bottles back into the freezer for next time, put the food way and wipe down and put in the garage to dry out.	✔
Life Jackets	Remove all life jackets and hang to air dry	✔

Cushions	Place all seat cushions in a way that will allow the entire boat to air dry. Wipe down any wet areas. Sometimes a wet-vacuum or carpet cleaner is great for vacuuming up the excess moisture in the carpets.	✔
Clean Boat	Wait, we already cleaned the boat at the boat ramp, so we are done. ☺	✔

4.4 Putting the Boat Away

Item	Note	Check
Cushions	Place all seat cushions in a way to allow the entire boat to air dry. Wipe down any wet areas. Use a wet vacuum or carpet cleaner to remove excess moisture in the carpets or bilge.	✔
Bilge	Remove the excess water from the bilge. Excess water in the bilge will lead to mildew and mold in the boat.	✔
Trailer	Jack the tongue of the trailer as high as possible to allow any water in the boat to drain out the rear. Especially important in the winter when raining.	✔
Battery Switch	Double check that the battery switch is off.	✔
Cover	During hot weather leave the cover off for a day to allow the boat to dry out. If it is raining or cool put the cover on to keep additional water out.	✔
Rest and Relax	Now that you are home and everything is put away and everyone had a great time; sit down, put your feet up and enjoy your favorite beverage.	✔

5 Important

5.1 Do NOT

Item	Note	Do NOT
Things to avoid	Here is a partial list of things to avoid.	🚫
Prep the boat on the Ramp	Prepare your boat for launching prior to getting on the boat ramp. .	🚫
Start the boat on the Ramp	DO NOT start your boat on the ramp. The raw water pump rubber impeller will be damaged and result in an over-heating engine.	🚫
Back down too fast	Backing down too fast may result in losing control due to water or oil on the boat ramp. It happens.	🚫
Pulling out too fast	Pulling the boat out too fast may break the winch line; boat land on the trailer in an inappropriate manner, or worse, slide off the trailer onto the ramp. It happens.	🚫
Unhook the boat from the trailer before getting to water	Never unhook the boat from trailer until the boat is over water. Your boat could slide off the trailer onto the concrete ramp. It happens.	🚫
Launch without the plug installed	It happens which is why it is a good idea to install the plug at home.	🚫
Drink Alcohol	Alcohol and boating DO NOT mix – Period.	🚫

Jump from a boat to the dock	Never jump from a boat to the dock. Allow the driver to dock the boat, stop all forward motion and then step off and tie off.	

5.2 Not Addressed

Item	Note	Check
Not Addressed	Here is a partial list of items not addressed in this checklist. Seek guidance for these subject matters.	✓
Winter Storage	Preparing the boat for winter storage is important. Seek a qualified marine service center.	✓
Regular Maintenance	Regular maintenance is important to maintain your investment and keep all the boating adventures fun.	✓
Incidents	Incidents and accidents requiring first aid, emergency services or towing services are not covered. Call 911 when appropriate and always have a first aid kit on the boat.	✓
Rules of the Road	Study the resources at the California Department of Boating and Waterways and from the United States Coast Guard.	✓

5.3 Definitions

Nautical definitions are easily accessible via the Internet and this abbreviated list from Wikipedia is included for people new to boating. It may seem unnecessary and even redundant, however, having a basic understanding of boating language is a safety issue. It is important to understand and speak the language of boating to be responsible and in safe command of your vessel. And it can be fun for the family to learn about the boat and what things are called. It is much better and more clear to cite the bilge pump versus that thingy.

The words highlighted in red are familiar terms for any boater. This abbreviated list from Wikipedia includes edits by yours truly.

A

Abandon ship!

> An imperative to leave the vessel immediately, usually in the face of some imminent overwhelming danger. It is an order issued by the Master or a delegated person in command. It is usually the last resort after all other mitigating actions have failed or become impossible, and destruction or loss of the ship is imminent; and customarily followed by a command to "man the lifeboats" or life rafts.

Admiral

> Senior naval officer of Flag rank. In ascending order of seniority, Rear Admiral, Vice Admiral, Admiral and Admiral of the Fleet (Royal Navy). Derivation Arabic, from *Amir al-Bahr* ("Ruler of the sea"). You may be the Driver or Captain, but your partner is the Admiral.

Adrift

> Afloat and unattached in any way to the shore or seabed, but not under way. It implies that a vessel is not under control and therefore goes where the wind and current take her.

Aft

> 1. The portion of the vessel behind the middle area of the vessel.
> 2. Towards the stern (of the vessel).

Aground

>Resting on or touching the ground or bottom (usually involuntarily).

Ahead

>Forward of the bow.

Ahoy

>A cry to draw attention. Term used to hail a boat or a ship, as "*Boat ahoy!*"

Aid to Navigation

>(ATON) Any device external to a vessel or aircraft specifically intended to assist navigators in determining their position or safe course, or to warn them of dangers or obstructions to navigation.

Amidships (or midships)

>In the middle portion of ship, along the line of the keel.

Anchor

>1. an object designed to prevent or slow the drift of a ship, attached to the ship by a line or chain; typically, a metal, hook-like or plough-like object designed to grip the bottom under the body of water (also see *sea anchor*).

Anchor ball

>Round black shape hoisted in the forepart of a vessel to show that it is anchored.

Anchor chain (or anchor cable)

>Chain connecting the ship to the anchor.

Anchor light

>White light displayed by a ship at anchor. Two such lights are displayed by a ship over 150 feet (46 m) in length.

Anchor rode

>The anchor line, rope or cable connecting the anchor chain to the vessel. Also Rode.

Anchorage

>A suitable place for a ship to anchor. Area of a port or harbor.

Astern

>1. Toward the stern (rear) of a vessel.
>
>2. Behind a vessel.

Aye, aye /ˌaɪ ˈaɪ/

Reply to an order or command to indicate that it, firstly, is heard; and, secondly, is understood and will be carried out. ("Aye, aye, sir" to officers). Also the proper reply from a hailed boat, to indicate that an officer is on board.

B

Bailer

A device for removing water that has entered the boat. Bucket

Batten down the hatches

To prepare for inclement weather by securing the closed hatch covers with wooden battens to prevent water from entering from any angle.

Beam

The width of a vessel at the widest point, or a point alongside the ship at the midpoint of its length.

Bearing

The horizontal direction of a line of sight between two objects on the surface of the earth. See also *absolute bearing* and *relative bearing*.

Bend

A knot used to join two ropes or lines. See also *hitch*.

Bight

1. Bight, a loop in rope or line—a hitch or knot tied *on the bight* is one tied in the middle of a rope, without access to the ends.
2. An indentation in a coastline.

Bilge

The compartment at the bottom of the hull of a ship or boat where water collects and must be pumped out of the vessel.

Bimini top

Open-front canvas top for the cockpit of a boat, usually supported by a metal frame.

Bitter end

The last part or loose end of a rope or cable. The anchor cable is tied to the bitts; when the cable is fully paid out, the bitter end has been reached.

Boat

> 1. A small craft or vessel designed to float on, and provide transport over, or under, water.
>
> 2. Naval term for a submarine of any size.

Boat-hook

> A pole with a hook on the end, used to reach into the water to catch buoys or other floating objects.

Bow

> The front of a vessel.

Bowline

> A type of knot, producing a strong loop of a fixed size, topologically similar to a sheet bend.

Breakwater

> A structure constructed on a coast as part of a coastal defense system or to protect an anchorage from the effects of weather.

Brightwork

> Exposed varnished wood or polished metal on a boat.

Bulkhead

> An upright wall within the hull of a ship. Particularly a watertight, load-bearing wall.

Buoy

> A floating object of defined shape and color, which is anchored at a given position and serves as an aid to navigation.

Burgee

> A small flag, typically triangular, flown from the masthead of a yacht to indicate yacht-club membership.

C

Capsize

> When a ship or boat lists too far and rolls over, exposing the keel. On large vessels, this often results in the sinking of the ship. Compare Turtling, infra.

Driver

> The person lawfully in command of a vessel. "Driver" is an informal title of respect given to the commander of a naval vessel regardless of his or her formal rank; aboard a merchant ship, the ship's *master* is her "Driver."

Chafing

Wear on line or sail caused by constant rubbing against another surface.

Chafing gear

Material applied to a line or spar to prevent or reduce chafing. See Baggywrinkle.

Chain locker

A space in the forward part of the ship, typically beneath the bow in front of the foremost collision bulkhead, that contains the anchor chain when the anchor is secured for sea.

Cleat

A stationary device used to secure a rope aboard a vessel.

Cockpit

The seating area (not to be confused with Deck). The area towards the stern of a small decked vessel that houses the rudder controls.

Compass

Navigational instrument showing the direction of the vessel in relation to the Earth's magnetic poles.

Cut and run

When wanting to make a quick escape, a ship might cut lashings to sails or cables for anchors, causing damage to the rigging, or losing an anchor, but shortening the time needed to make ready by bypassing the proper procedures.

Cut of his jib

The "cut" of a sail refers to its shape. Since this would vary between ships, it could be used both to identify a familiar vessel at a distance, and to judge the possible sailing qualities of an unknown one. Also used figuratively of people.[14]

D

Day beacon

An unlighted fixed structure which is equipped with a day board for daytime identification.

Dead ahead

Exactly ahead, directly ahead, directly in front.

Dead in the water

Not moving (used only when a vessel is afloat and neither tied up nor anchored).

Displacement

The weight of water displaced by the immersed volume of a ship's hull, exactly equivalent to the weight of the whole ship.

Displacement hull

A hull designed to travel through the water, rather than planing over it. Most small powerboats have planing hulls

Dock

1. A fixed structure attached to shore to which a vessel is secured when in port, generally synonymous with *pier* and *wharf*, except that *pier* tends to refer to structures used for tying up commercial ships and to structures extending from shore for use in fishing, while *dock* refers more generally to facilities used for tying up ships or boats, including recreational craft.

Doldrums or equatorial calms

The equatorial trough, with special reference to the light and variable nature of the winds.[17]

Draft or draught (both /ˈdrɑːft/)

The depth of a ship's keel below the waterline.

E

Extremis

(also known as "in extremis") the point under International Rules of the Road (Navigation Rules) at which the privileged (or stand-on) vessel on collision course with a burdened (or give-way) vessel determines it must maneuver to avoid a collision. Prior to extremis, the privileged vessel must maintain course and speed and the burdened vessel must maneuver to avoid collision.

Eye splice

A closed loop or eye at the end a line, rope, cable etc. It is made by unraveling its end and joining it to itself by intertwining it into the lay of the line. Eye splices are very strong and compact and are employed in moorings and docking lines among other uses.

F

Fair winds and following seas

A blessing wishing the recipient a safe journey and good fortune.

Fantail

Aft end of the ship, also known as the Poop deck.

Fast

Fastened or held firmly (*fast aground*: stuck on the seabed; *made fast*: tied securely).

Fathom /ˈfæðəm/

A unit of length equal to 6 feet (1.8 m), roughly measured as the distance between a man's outstretched hands. Particularly used to measure depth.

Fender

An air or foam filled bumper used in boating to keep boats from banging into docks or each other.

Fetch

1. The distance across water which a wind or waves have traveled.
2. To reach a mark without tacking.

Fid

1. A tapered wooden tool used for separating the strands of rope for splicing.
2. A bar used to fix an upper mast in place.

First mate

The second-in-command of a commercial ship.

Fixed propeller

A propeller mounted on a rigid shaft protruding from the hull of a vessel, usually driven by an inboard motor; steering must be done using a rudder.

Flotsam

Debris or cargo that remains afloat after a shipwreck. See also jetsam.

Fluke

The wedge-shaped part of an anchor's arms that digs into the bottom.

Following sea
Wave or tidal movement going in the same direction as a ship

Freeboard
The height of a ship's hull (excluding superstructure) above the waterline. The vertical distance from the current waterline to the lowest point on the highest continuous watertight deck. This usually varies from one part to another.

G

Gangplank
A movable bridge used in boarding or leaving a ship at a pier; also known as a "brow".

Give-way (vessel)
Where two vessels are approaching one another so as to involve a risk of collision, this is the vessel which is directed to keep out of the way of the other.

Global Positioning System
(GPS) A satellite based navigation system providing continuous worldwide coverage. It provides navigation, position, and timing information to air, marine, and land users.

Grounding
When a ship (while afloat) touches the bed of the sea, or goes "aground" (q.v.).

Gunwale /'gun əl/
Upper edge of the hull.

H

Halyard or halliard
Originally, ropes used for hoisting a spar with a sail attached; today, a line used to raise the head of any sail.

Harbor
A harbor or harbour, or haven, is a place where ships may shelter from the weather or are stored. Harbors can be man-made or natural.

Hard

A section of otherwise muddy shoreline suitable for mooring or hauling out.

Hawsepipe, hawsehole or hawse

The shaft or hole in the side of a vessel's bow through which the anchor chain passes.

Head

1. The forward most or uppermost portion of the ship.
2. The toilet of a vessel, which in sailing ships projected from the bows and therefore was located in the "head" of the vessel.

Helm

A ship's steering mechanism; see tiller and ship's wheel. The wheel and/or wheelhouse area. See also *wheelhouse*.

Helmsman

A person who steers a ship.

Hitch

A knot used to tie a rope or line to a fixed object. Also see *bend*.

I

In irons

When the bow of a sailboat is headed into the wind and the boat has stalled and is unable to maneuver.

Inboard motor

An engine mounted within the hull of a vessel, usually driving a fixed propeller by a shaft protruding through the stern. Generally used on larger vessels. See also *sterndrive* and *outboard motor*.

Inboard-Outboard drive system

See *sterndrive*.

Iron wind

What sailors call inboard engines.

J

Jetsam

Debris ejected from a ship that sinks or washes ashore. See also Flotsam.

K

Keel

> The central structural basis of the hull in traditional shipbuilding. The keel is also the lowest centerline structure of the hull in the water.

Keelhauling

> Maritime punishment: to punish by dragging a person under the keel of a ship.

Kissing the gunner's daughter

> Bending over the barrel of a gun for punitive beating with a cane or cat.

Knot

> A unit of speed: 1 nautical mile (1.1508 mi, 6076.1 ft) per hour. A statue mail is 5280 feet. Originally speed was measured by paying out a line from the stern of a moving boat; the line had a knot every 47 feet 3 inches, and the number of knots passed out in 30 seconds gave the speed through the water in nautical miles per hour. Sometimes "knots" is mistakenly stated as "knots per hour," but the latter is a measure of acceleration (i.e., "nautical miles per hour per hour") rather than of speed.

L

Ladder

> On board a ship, all "stairs" are called ladders, except for literal staircases aboard passenger ships. Most "stairs" on a ship are narrow and nearly vertical, hence the name. Believed to be from the Anglo-Saxon word hiaeder, meaning ladder.

Land lubber

> A person unfamiliar with being on the sea.

Lazaret (also Lazarette or Lazaretto)

> A small stowage locker at the aft end of a boat.

League

> A unit of length, normally equal to three nautical miles.

Lee side

> The side of a ship sheltered from the wind (cf. weather side).

Length overall, or LOA

> The maximum length of a vessel's hull measured parallel to the waterline, usually measured on the hull alone, and including

overhanging ends that extend beyond the main bow and main stern perpendicular members. For sailing vessels, this may exclude the bowsprit and other fittings added to the hull, but sometimes bowsprits are included.

Lifeboat

1. Shipboard lifeboat, kept on board a vessel and used to take crew and passengers to safety in the event of the ship being abandoned.
2. Rescue lifeboat, usually launched from shore, used to rescue people from the water or from vessels in difficulty.

Liferaft

An inflatable, covered raft, used in the event of a vessel being abandoned.

Line

The correct nautical term for the majority of the cordage or "ropes" used on a vessel.

List

A vessel's angle of lean or tilt to one side, in the direction called roll. Typically refers to a lean caused by flooding or improperly loaded or shifted cargo (as opposed to 'heeling', which see).

Loose cannon

An irresponsible and reckless individual whose behavior (either intended or unintended) endangers the group he or she belongs. A loose cannon, weighing thousands of pounds, would crush anything and anyone in its path, and possibly even break a hole in the hull, thus endangering the seaworthiness of the whole ship.

M

Magnetic bearing

An absolute bearing (q.v.) using magnetic north. Not the same as the geographic North Pole.

Magnetic north

The direction towards the North Magnetic Pole. Varies slowly over time.

Main deck

The uppermost continuous deck extending from bow to stern.

Making way
>When a vessel is moving under its own power.

Man overboard!
>A cry let out when a seaman has gone 'overboard' (fallen from the ship into the water).

Marina
>A docking facility for small ships and yachts.

Marlinspike
>A tool used in ropework for tasks such as unlaying rope for splicing, untying knots, or forming a makeshift handle.

Master
>The Driver of a commercial vessel.

Monkey's fist
>A ball woven out of line used to provide heft to heave the line to another location. The monkey fist and other heaving-line knots were sometimes weighted with lead.

M.V. (or MV)
>Prefix for "Motor Vessel", used before a ship's name.

N

Nautical mile
>A unit of length corresponding approximately to one minute of arc of latitude along any meridian arc. By international agreement it is exactly 1,852 meters (approximately 6,076.1 feet).

Navigation rules
>Rules of the road that provide guidance on how to avoid collision and also used to assign blame when a collision does occur.

Nay
>"no"; the opposite of "aye".

No room to swing a cat
>The entire ship's company was expected to witness floggings, assembled on deck. If it was very crowded, the bosun might not have room to swing the "cat o' nine tails" (the whip).

Nun

A type of navigational buoy often cone shaped, but if not, always triangular in silhouette, colored green. In channel marking its use is opposite that of a "can buoy".

O

Old man, (The)

Crew's slang for the Driver (master or commanding officer) of a vessel.

Old salt

Slang for an experienced mariner.

On the hard

A boat that has been hauled and is now sitting on dry land.

Outboard motor

A motor mounted externally on the transom of a small boat. The boat may be steered by twisting the whole motor, instead of or in addition to using a rudder.

Outdrive

The lower part of a sterndrive (*q.v.*).

bared), with a cane or cat, while bending, often tied down, over the barrel of a gun, known as #Kissing the gunner's daughter.

P

Painter

A rope attached to the bow of a dinghy, usually used to tow dingy or handle it at dockside, or in water.

Parley

A discussion or conference, especially between enemies, over terms of a truce or other matters.

Pier

A raised structure, typically supported by widely spread piles or pillars. Non floating.

Pipe down

A signal on the bosun's pipe to signal the end of the day, requiring lights (and smoking pipes) to be extinguished and silence from the crew.

Pitch

A vessel's motion, rotating about the beam/transverse axis, causing the fore and aft ends to rise and fall repetitively.

Pitchpole

To capsize a boat stern over bow, rather than by rolling over.

Plane

To skim over the water at high speed rather than push through it.

Point

A unit of bearing equal to one thirty-second of a circle, i.e., 11.25°. A turn of 32 points is a complete turn through 360°.

Port

The left side of the boat. Towards the left-hand side of the ship facing forward (formerly Larboard). Denoted with a red light at night.

Propeller (fixed)

A propeller mounted on a rigid shaft protruding from the hull of a vessel, usually driven by an inboard motor;

Propeller walk or prop walk

Tendency for a propeller to push the stern sideways. In theory a right-hand propeller in reverse will walk the stern to port.

Q

Quarterdeck

The aftermost deck of a warship. In the age of sail, the quarterdeck was the preserve of the ship's officers.

R

Ram

1. To intentionally collide with another vessel with the intention of damaging or sinking her.
2. To accidentally collide bow-first with another vessel.

Range lights

Two lights associated to form a range (a line formed by the extension of a line connecting two charted points) which often, but not necessarily, indicates the channel centerline. The front range light is the lower of the two, and nearer to the mariner using the range. The rear light is higher and further from the mariner.

Reef

1. Reefing: To temporarily reduce the area of a sail exposed to the wind, usually to guard against adverse effects of strong wind or to slow the vessel.
2. Reef: Rock or coral, possibly only revealed at low tide, shallow enough that the vessel will at least touch if not go aground.

Reefer

1. A shipboard refrigerator.

Regatta

A series of boat races, usually of sailboats or rowboats, but occasionally of powered boats.

Relative bearing

A bearing relative to the direction of the ship: the clockwise angle between the ship's direction and an object. If the relative bearing between you and the other vessel, a collision course is in the making.

Rode

The anchor line, rope or cable connecting the anchor chain to the vessel. Also Anchor Rode.

Rudder

A steering device which can be placed aft, externally relative to the keel or compounded into the keel either independently or as part of the bulb/centerboard.

Running gear

The propellers, shafts, struts and related parts of a motorboat.

S

Safe harbor

A harbor which provides safety from bad weather

Sampson post

A strong vertical post used to support a ship's windlass and the heel of a ship's bowsprit.

Screw

1. Propeller.

2. Propeller-driven (e.g., screw frigate, screw sloop).

Scuppers

Originally a series of pipes fitted through the ships side from inside the thicker deck waterway to the topside planking to drain water overboard, larger quantities drained through freeing ports, which were openings in the bulwarks.

Scuttlebutt

1. A barrel with a hole in used to hold water that sailors would drink from. By extension (in modern naval usage), a shipboard drinking fountain or water cooler.

2. Slang for gossip.

Shakedown cruise

A cruise performed before a ship enters service or after major changes such as a crew change, repair, or overhaul during which the performance of the ship and her crew are tested under working conditions.

Shanghaied

Condition of a crewman involuntarily impressed into service on a ship.

Skeg

A downward or sternward projection from the keel in front of the rudder. Protects the rudder from damage.

Driver

The Driver of a ship.

Slop chest

A ship's store of merchandise, such as clothing, tobacco, etc., maintained aboard merchant ships for sale to the crew.

SOG

Speed over ground, speed of the vessel relative to the Earth (and as shown by a GPS). Referenced on many fishing forums.

Spring

A line used parallel to that of the length of a craft, to prevent fore-aft motion of a boat, when moored or docked.

Splice

To join lines (ropes, cables etc.) by unravelling their ends and intertwining them to form a continuous line. To form an eye or a knot by splicing.

S.S. (or SS)

Prefix for "Steam Ship", used before a ship's name.

Stanchion

vertical post near a deck's edge that supports life-lines. A timber fitted in between the frame heads on a wooden hull or a bracket on a steel vessel, approximately one meter high, to support the bulwark plank or plating and the rail.

Stand-on (vessel)

A vessel directed to keep her course and speed where two vessels are approaching one another so as to involve a risk of collision.

Starboard

The right side of the boat. Towards the right-hand side of a vessel facing forward. Denoted with a green light at night. Derived from the old steering oar or *steerboard* which preceded the invention of the rudder.

Stern

The rear part of a ship, technically defined as the area built up over the sternpost, extending upwards from the counter rail to the taffrail.

Stern tube

1. The tube under the hull to bear the tailshaft for propulsion (usually at stern).
2. A torpedo tube mounted in the stern of a submarine.

Sterndrive

A propeller drive system similar to the lower part of an outboard motor extending below the hull of a larger power boat or yacht, but driven by an engine mounted within the hull. Unlike a fixed propeller (but like an outboard), the boat may be steered by twisting the drive. Also see *inboard motor* and *outboard motor*.

Stopper knot

A knot tied in the end of a rope, usually to stop it passing through a hole; most commonly a figure-eight knot.

Stow

to store, or to put away e.g. personal effects, tackle, or cargo.

STW

Speed through (the) water, speed of the vessel relative to the surrounding water (and as shown by a <u>Log</u>). Used in navigation.

T

Tack

1. A leg of the route of a sailing vessel, particularly in relation to *tacking (q.v.)* and to *starboard tack* and *port tack* (also *q.v.*).
2. The front bottom corner of a sail.

<u>*Tell-tale*</u> *(sometimes tell-tail)*

A light piece of string, yarn, rope or plastic (often magnetic audio tape) attached to a <u>stay</u> or a <u>shroud</u> to indicate the local wind direction. Also placed on sails to provide a visual indicator when trimming sails.

Three sheets to the wind

On a three-masted ship, having the sheets of the three lower courses loose will result in the ship meandering aimlessly downwind. Also, a sailor who has drunk strong spirits beyond his capacity.

<u>*Tiller*</u>

A lever used for steering, attached to the top of the rudder post.

<u>*Transom*</u>

The aft "wall" of the stern; often the part to which an outboard unit or the drive portion of a sterndrive is attached.

<u>*True north*</u>

The direction of the geographical <u>North Pole</u> which is not the magnetic North Pole.

U

Under way or underway

A vessel that is moving under control: that is, neither at anchor, made fast to the shore, aground nor adrift.

Underwater hull or underwater ship

The underwater section of a vessel beneath the waterline, normally not visible except when in drydock.

V

V-hull

The shape of a boat or ship in which the contours of the hull come in a straight line to the keel.

W

Wake

Turbulence behind a vessel. Not to be confused with *wash*.

Wash

The waves created by a vessel. Not to be confused with *wake*.

Waterline

The line where the hull of a ship meets the water's surface.

Waterway

Waterway, a navigable body of water.

Way

Speed, progress, or momentum. To *make way* is to move; to *lose way* is to slow down.

Waypoint

A location defined by navigational coordinates, especially as part of a planned route.

Weather side

The side of a ship exposed to the wind.

Weigh anchor

To heave up (an anchor) preparatory to sailing.

Well

Place in the ship's hold for pumps.

Wheel *or ship's wheel*

The usual steering device on larger vessels: a wheel with a horizontal axis, connected by cables to the rudder.

Wheelhouse

Location on a ship where the wheel is located; also called pilothouse or bridge.

Windage

Wind resistance of the boat.

Windlass

A winch mechanism, where mechanical advantage greater than that obtainable by block and tackle is needed such as raising the anchor.

Windward

In the direction that the wind is coming from.

Y

Yacht

A recreational boat or ship; the term includes *sailing yachts*, *motor yachts*, and *steam yachts*. Larger than 26 feet.

Yarr

Acknowledgement of an order, or agreement. Also *aye, aye*.

Yaw

A vessel's rotational motion about the vertical axis, causing the fore and aft ends to swing from side to side repetitively.

Happy Boating!

Printed in Great Britain
by Amazon